THE **NORWEGIANS** IN AMERICA

THE NORWEGIANS
IN AMERICA

Percie V. Hillbrand

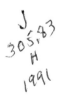

 Lerner Publications Company · Minneapolis

Front cover: Three friends from Minneapolis, Minnesota, celebrate Norwegian Independence Day in traditional Norwegian costumes. The women on the left and right wear dresses from Norway's Telemark County, and the woman in the center wears a dress from Møre og Romsdal County.

Page 2: Skiers in the American Birkebeiner race stream down Main Street in Hayward, Wisconsin. The 34-mile (55-kilometer) marathon is the most popular cross-country ski race in North America, attracting over 6,000 competitors each year. It is named after the Birkebeiner Rennet, a cross-country ski race held in Norway.

1991 REVISED EDITION

The Library of Congress cataloged the original printing of this title as follows:

Hillbrand, Percie V.
    The Norwegians in America. Minneapolis, Lerner Publications Co. [1967]

    79 p. illus., maps, ports. 24 cm. (The In America Series)

    Briefly describes the land and people of Norway, chronicles the early Viking explorations and settlements in the U.S. and surveys the Norwegian contributions to American life and culture in various areas.

    1. Norwegians in the U.S. — Juvenile literature. I. Title.

E184.S2H55   301.453′481′073   67-15683
ISBN 0-8225-0243-7 [Library]
ISBN 0-8225-1041-3 [Paper]

Manufactured in the United States of America

7   8   9   10   11   12   13   14   15   99   98   97   96   95   94   93   92   91

CONTENTS

1
DISCOVERING AMERICA

Many scholars believe that Leif Ericson was the European discoverer of North America. Leif's explorations were not well documented, however, and his discovery cannot be supported by fact.

A Nation of Travelers

The Norwegian Americans descend from a long line of world travelers. From about A.D. 800 to 1050, Norse Vikings sailed to Great Britain, France, Italy, and Spain, as well as to Russia, Iceland, Greenland, and North America. In the 17th century, thousands of Norwegians migrated from Norway to the Netherlands. In the 19th century, hundreds of thousands moved to the United States.

A variety of circumstances, both political and economic, set off each migratory wave. Overcrowding and a shortage of farmland were the most common calamities that forced Norwegians to leave their homes. Norway's mountain ranges run the full length of the country from north to south. The northern third of Norway lies above

6

Arnold, Arlyss, and Lori Olsen–a Norwegian-American family from Minneapolis, Minnesota

the Arctic Circle, where the growing season is extremely short. Altogether, only 3 to 4 percent of Norway's land is suitable for farming. For centuries rural Norwegians were frustrated and defeated by the geographic limitations of their homeland.

By the early 1800s, as reports reached the Norwegians of cheap, unsettled land in North America, many were eager for a new beginning. They began to leave their country in large numbers for life in the American Midwest. The departure from Norway began in 1825, picked up speed throughout the 1840s, and became a mass exodus in 1866, when approximately 15,500 Norwegians left their country in one year alone. Most of the emigrants headed for the United States.

Between 1866 and 1915, during the peak of the emigration, over 600,000 Norwegians went to America. The loss was devastating to Norway. No other country except Ireland lost more of its people to the United States. The U.S. Census Bureau reported that, in 1980, about 3.5 million U.S. residents claimed Norwegian ancestry–a number nearly equal to the population of Norway that year.

While the numbers are startling from a Norwegian perspective, the Norwegian-American population has never made up more than 2 percent of the total population of the United States. Yet the Norwegian-American presence has had a strong impact. Some of America's great educators, political leaders, scientists, and writers have been of Norwegian descent.

Vikings carved animal heads on the tops of posts to protect themselves from evil spirits. This animal head post, dating from about A.D. 850, was found in Norway in the burial ship of a Viking queen.

Viking Voyages

Legend has commonly portrayed the Vikings, or early Scandinavians, as invaders and plunderers. It is true that some did go on rampages, and that during the early 800s bands of Vikings invaded Great Britain and Ireland. During the mid-800s, they struck France, Italy, and Spain. Conquering foreign lands was the surest means of obtaining wealth and honor in the Viking culture. The reason for most invasions, however, was a shortage of land in Norway.

Despite their reputation as warriors, most Vikings lived peaceful lives. The majority supported themselves through farming and fishing. Recent archaeological finds suggest that many Vikings were explorers and traders—some journeyed regularly across the Atlantic.

Most of what we know of the Vikings comes from the prose narratives, called sagas, of early Icelandic writers. The sagas tell stories of heroic Vikings —either of fact or of legend. Though the stories take place from the time of the Viking settlement of Iceland (in about 870), to the time that Christianity came to Iceland (in 1000), the sagas were written centuries later. From the 13th century, about three dozen "family sagas" survive, among them the "Saga of Eric the Red" and the "Saga of the Greenlanders," which tell the story of Eric the Red and his son, Leif Ericson.

Eric the Red discovered Greenland and established a colony there on the southwest coast.

Eric Thorvaldson, called Eric the Red because of his red hair, moved to Iceland at the age of 10 when his father was banished from Norway on charges of manslaughter. Years later, criminal charges were brought against Eric, and he was banished from Iceland for three years. He went to sea—sailing westward, hoping to find the land that a Norwegian sailor had sighted many years before. Eric found the land and settled there for the remainder of his banishment. Determined to return someday with other settlers, he named the land "Greenland" to make it sound attractive.

Soon after his return to Norway, in about 985, Eric led a fleet of 25 ships toward Greenland. Only 14 ships and about 400 people safely reached the island, but a Viking colony quickly took root. By the year 1000, Greenland had approximately 1000 Viking settlers. An epidemic around 1002 killed many of these original colonists, including Eric himself. But Eric's son, Leif, grew to adulthood in Greenland. The original colony survived, and settlers founded new colonies in the area.

The two sagas continue to tell the story of Leif, but they differ greatly in

Borgund stave (wooden) church, built in 1138, is one of the best preserved of the early Christian churches in Norway. The structure is adorned with a combination of Viking motifs (including dragon heads) and the Christian symbol of the cross.

their reports. According to the "Saga of Eric," Leif spent a winter in Norway, at age 19, where he was converted to Christianity. The following spring, Norway's king assigned Leif to establish Christianity among his fellow settlers in Greenland. On his voyage home, Leif's ship went off course, and he came to a land of which he had no previous knowledge. The country was rich with wild grapes, so when Leif returned to Greenland, he called the new land "Vinland," or "Wine Land."

The "Saga of the Greenlanders" tells a different story. According to this report, a Norse Viking sea captain named Bjarni Jerolfsson was driven off his course on a voyage from Norway to Greenland in the year 986. He landed on a strange new land and then sailed to Greenland, where he told the people about his discovery. Leif Ericson became interested in this story. With a ship and 35 men Leif sailed south and west, and he reached the new land, which he later named "Vinland."

Shortly after Leif Ericson's discovery, this saga also says, a man named Thorfinn Thordarson, nicknamed Karlsefne, led an expedition to find

Vinland. Bringing livestock and farming equipment, the travelers made a settlement that lasted for about three years. Hostilities broke out with the Native Americans, and the Norse settlers returned to Greenland.

Scholars believe the "Saga of the Greenlanders" to be the older and more authentic story. No findings can confirm either saga, however, and other Icelandic sources mention Leif Ericson without stating that he discovered Vinland. Still others tell of Vinland without mention of Leif. No known maps exist to confirm the site of Vinland, though scholars believe it might have been located in Cape Cod, Massachusetts, in northern Maine, or in Newfoundland, Canada.

In the late 19th century, the controversy of early Scandinavian settlements reached its peak. Many people went to the press with dozens of suspicious "Viking" artifacts. The most famous is the Kensington runestone, reportedly unearthed by Olof Ohman, a Swedish immigrant, on his farm in Kensington, Minnesota. An inscription on the stone is dated 1362, but linguists consider the find a hoax. The phrasing is atypical of Scandinavian languages of the 1300s, they say, and bears a curious resemblance to modern Swedish.

An important 20th-century discovery is that of Norwegian explorer Helge Ingstad and his wife, Anne Stine Ingstad, an archaeologist. In 1960, the Ingstads began exploring an area near the fishing village of L'Anse aux Meadows, at the northernmost tip of Newfoundland. The area where they dug was known locally as an "Indian camp." Newfoundland villagers had long supposed that the mounds of earth covered a Native American burial ground. The Ingstads made a different discovery – the long, rectangular ridges under the earth were the ruins of a building's foundation. The ruins matched those of ancient Norse structures in Greenland.

In 1963 the Ingstads announced the results of their excavation, claiming

The Kensington runestone

Excavation of a Norse settlement at L'Anse aux Meadows, Newfoundland, was begun by Norwegian explorer Helge Ingstad and continued for several years under the direction of the Canadian Parks Service. The seven sod houses that were uncovered would have accommodated between 60 and 90 people.

the site to be the ruins of a 12th-century Norse settlement. Further investigations of the site brought up various tools that proved the settlement to be Norse. What archaeology cannot determine is whether the settlement at L'Anse aux Meadows is Leif Ericson's Vinland, or if Vinland was indeed farther south, where wild grapes grow. Leif Ericson may or may not have been the very first, but the excavations proved that the Norwegians were in North America long before Columbus's voyages.

Rediscovery

Other 20th-century findings have placed Norse settlements throughout Arctic Canada, in the Northwest Territories and in Newfoundland. Viking artifacts have been discovered on Ellesmere and Baffin islands, which suggests that the Vikings may have traded with the Inuit people.

The Viking settlements did not survive, however, most likely because of economic forces. Exploration in Africa and European trade with the East began in the 13th and 14th centuries. The furs and ivory that were the bulk of the Norse Vikings' trade were no longer in demand. The Vikings left North America, and memories of Vinland died, except among the few scholars who studied the saga manuscripts.

When an economic decline around the year 1500 prompted many Norwegians to find work outside Norway, most went to the Netherlands. Church records from the time tell us that thousands of Norwegians were registered as members of Lutheran congregations in Amsterdam and other Dutch cities. Most of the men were sailors who found jobs with the Dutch merchant marine or navy. Most of the women worked as servants.

Of the Norwegians who went to the Netherlands, a few eventually found their way to Dutch colonies in America —New Amsterdam, which became New York in 1663, Albany, and Schenectady. These Norwegians have remained virtually unnoticed in American colonial history, however, because they absorbed Dutch culture, intermarried, adopted the Dutch language, and changed the spelling of their names.

Until the end of the 18th century, most Norwegians probably knew little if anything about America and the European colonies there. Norway's mountain ranges separated the country from the rest of Europe, and Norwegians seldom received news of events outside their own country. As

A restored sod house at the L'Anse aux Meadows excavation site

Norwegians developed foreign trade markets, they began to hear news from across the Atlantic. They heard of the rebellion of the American colonies and the war for independence. They noticed similarities between the Americans' struggles and their own political struggles under the rule of Denmark and Sweden.

2
THE JOURNEY TO INDEPENDENCE

During his reign from 1015 to 1030, King Olav II forced Norwegians to convert to Christianity. While Norwegians once viewed him as a tyrant, they now honor him for bringing the Christian faith to their country.

Four Centuries under Denmark

When King Haakon VI died in 1380, he was to be the last ruler of an independent Norway for the next 400 years. The reign fell to his wife, Margrete, who was also the Danish ruler at the time, and in 1388 Swedish nobles elected her to rule their nation as well. Margrete united Norway, Denmark, and Sweden under the Union of Kalmar. Her power was centered in Denmark, however, and Norway and Sweden soon fell into neglect. After a series of struggles, Sweden eventually broke away from the union in 1523, but in 1536 Denmark was able to declare the severely weakened Norway a province.

The Norwegians deeply resented Denmark's intrusion into their lives, particularly in matters that affected them daily, such as their ways of worship. Not only did Denmark replace Catholicism with Lutheranism as the official religion of Norway, but the Danish language was also used in sermons, hymns, and scripture. As a

The interior of a stave church that was built in Norway during the 1100s

consequence of the four centuries of Danish rule, two new forms of the Norwegian language developed. A form called *bokmal* first replaced Old Norse. Actually a "Norwegianized" form of Danish, it employs Danish vocabulary and spelling, but it is pronounced very differently. New Norwegian, or *nynorsk,* is a language that was created in the mid-1800s as a reaction against the Danish influence. It was based on the many local forms of speech that developed in the villages during the union of Norway and Denmark.

As the 19th century began, Norway was feeling the effects of war. Napoleon's rampage across Europe left the Norwegians destitute. While Denmark became an ally of France against Great Britain, Britain cut off trade with Norway. British warships also blocked Norway's trade with other countries, and many Norwegians starved.

Trade blocks were lifted and Norway's economy improved when Sweden, an ally of Britain, defeated Denmark in 1813. Yet Norway was to face another obstacle when, according to the 1814 agreement called the Treaty of Kiel, Denmark gave Norway to Sweden.

The Norwegians didn't recognize the treaty. They instead elected an assembly to draw up a constitution for an independent nation and adopted the constitution on May 17, 1814. Sweden refused to grant Norway independence, however, and Swedish forces attacked and defeated Norwegian troops. King Charles XIII of Sweden promised to respect the Norwegian constitution and granted Norway much internal independence, but Sweden still controlled Norway's foreign affairs.

As Norwegians gradually learned of events in America, they developed a keen interest in the new country. America promised universal voting rights—at least for men, at that point in U.S. history. (The right to vote was not extended to all Norwegian men until 1898.) America had no official class, as Norway did. America also

Eidsvoll Manor, where Norway's constitution was signed on May 17, 1814. The building is now a historical museum.

Johan Sverdrup did much to weaken the union between Sweden and Norway. He served in the Norwegian parliament for many years, and he became prime minister of Norway in 1884. As founder of the Venstre (liberal) party, he united rural Norwegians and encouraged them to speak up for their needs.

appealed to Lutherans who wanted to practice their faith under less restrictive conditions and to religious nonconformists of all kinds.

Of all the factors that pushed the Norwegians to emigrate, the strongest were economic. Norway's export industries in mining, lumbering, fishing, and shipping grew steadily throughout the 19th century. Farmers were able to modernize production and move into commercial agriculture. Yet advances in health care during this period meant that people were healthier and living longer, and the economy could not keep pace with the expanding population. The distribution of the new wealth was also uneven, and the bottom stratum of society grew.

In the 1860s, Norway saw an agricultural crisis. Farmers who had invested heavily in modernizing production lost their domestic markets to cheap imported grain. Many of the farmers who were forced to switch over to cattle raising did not survive the transition and went bankrupt. This situation aggravated an older problem. Farms in Norway were still subject to an old Viking law granting land rights to the male head of a family. When a farmer died, no subdivision of his land was allowed. The oldest son inherited all his father's property, and his brothers and sisters were left with nothing.

In the 1880s, Norway's economy stagnated, and a new force of young workers faced bleak employment prospects. As Norway's population continued to grow, the reasons for going to America kept building.

A farmhouse in Telemark, Norway, built in about 1750. Like many rural Norwegian structures of this period, it is sparsely furnished, yet elaborate wood carving and rosemaling (rose painting) add warmth to the home.

Sloopers

Though they became devout Lutherans, many Norwegians were discontented with what they perceived as worldliness within the clergy. In the early 19th century, Hans Nielsen Hauge, a man from the peasant class, stirred up a religious revival. Hauge traveled from one community to the next preaching his message. He did not call for people to leave the state church, but only to renew Christian life within

its framework. Yet Norway's church and government felt threatened by Hauge's ministry and he was put in prison. They could not restrain his influence, however, and Hauge gained many followers, called Haugeans.

Quakerism also found its way to Norway, via Norwegian prisoners of war in England during Napoleon's reign in Europe. Both the Quakers and Haugeans opposed the authority of the Norwegian state church. They both desired religious freedom and the right of lay people to preach the word of God. Although they had many fundamentally different beliefs, these similar positions drew them together.

In 1821 a group of Quakers and Haugeans convened in Stavanger, Norway. Having heard rumors of freedom of worship in the United States, they elected a man named Cleng Peerson to go to New York as their agent.

Peerson had traveled extensively in England, France, and Germany and was to be as great a traveler in America. The most influential leader of the emigrants in the early stages of the movement, Peerson has been called "the father of emigration." In 1824 he returned to Norway from his first trip to America, bringing with him a favorable report on prospects for emigration. Later the same year, he went back to America, visited western New York with a land agent, and agreed to purchase six pieces of land for the group of Quakers and Haugeans in Stavanger.

In July 1825, a party of 52 passengers and crew members altogether—all of whom intended to emigrate—sailed from Norway. There were 10 married couples with 19 children among them, 12 single men, and 1 single woman. Their small vessel, a sloop named *Restauration,* carried a cargo of iron that they would sell in New York. Peerson met the settlers—now numbering 53 after the birth of a baby girl during the 14-week voyage—and he led them to western New York, where they settled near Lake Ontario. These settlers, who became known as the "Sloopers," were forerunners of the mass emigration.

America Letters and America Books

After the Sloopers left Norway in 1825, there was no group emigration for another 10 years. The urge to leave Norway continued to grow, however, as the settlers wrote letters to their family and friends in Norway. The letters described the fertile land and the air of freedom in the United States. These first immigrants did not encounter much prejudice, and many were amazed by the absence of class distinctions in America. They wrote home about a wonderful country where any poor person could achieve wealth through hard work.

These reports, which came to be known as the "America Letters," were widely circulated. People sent the letters from farm to farm and from town to town. The letters became important news, and village newspapers printed many of the letters. Not all the letters were enthusiastic. Some told of hardships, such as epidemics of disease. Yet they broadened the imaginations of the Norwegians and bred wanderlust. For many, the letters were the first evidence of a real place called the United States of America.

Soon books were published in Norway for those who sought advice about emigration. Two guidebooks that were widely read were Ole Rynning's *True Account of America,* published in 1838, and Johan R. Reiersen's *Pathfinder for Norse Emigrants to the United North American States and Texas,* published in 1844. Rynning, a young man from the upper class, sympathized with Norway's disadvantaged farmers and laborers and wanted to help them emigrate. Reiersen acted as an agent for organized groups of emigrants who wanted reports on conditions in the United States.

The books gave advice such as the best time to leave Norway (spring) in order to reach a settlement in time for summer planting. People took the advice seriously, and March, April, and May became the months of heaviest emigration. The guides also advised travelers about what to take on the

A group poses to have its photograph taken before leaving Norway for the United States.

journey and what to expect on the ocean voyage. Rynning's book answered questions he had heard Norwegians ask about the United States, such as "What language is spoken in America? Is it difficult to learn?" and "Is it true that those who are taken to America are sold as slaves?"

Ships became more seaworthy in the 19th century, an improvement that made many people more willing to take a 10- to 14-week voyage across the Atlantic Ocean. The Sloopers had to buy their own boat, and other early emigrants had to travel to ports outside of Norway to find a ship headed for America. As talk of emigration increased, Norwegian ship captains realized the benefits of combining emigrant traffic with shipments of trade cargo. A fleet of ships for emigration eventually became available.

Letters and other writings tell us that most emigrants weren't joyful when they left their homes, or even especially hopeful. They studied the problems that faced them in Norway and read the reports from their friends and relatives in America. Carefully considering the prospects for themselves and their children in each country, they made their decision to leave.

This brother and sister left Norway in about 1900. They settled in Minnesota.

3
SETTLING IN

Norwegian Americans across the country celebrate Norwegian Independence Day, called **Syttende Mai** *(the 17th of May).*

Early Communities

Illinois, Wisconsin, and Iowa

The 53 Sloopers, in their settlement named Kendall, bought land for $5 an acre. The price seemed fair at the time of the purchase, but the land proved very difficult to clear. The settlers were unable to start farming for several years, and they consequently suffered from poor nutrition and disease. The settlement eventually took root, however, and prospered.

Despite the success of the Kendall colony, the settlers' agent, Cleng Peerson, began to look for new land. He suspected that cheaper land could be found west of New York and that the holdings in Kendall could be sold for a profit. In 1833 he set out on foot, and he explored the areas that are now Milwaukee and Chicago.

Peerson found good land. A particular site on the Fox River in Illinois was priced under $2 an acre, and the prairie with few trees looked easy to cultivate. Back in Kendall, Peerson

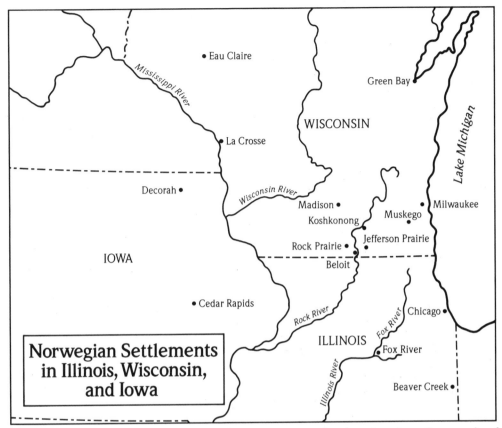

Norwegian Settlements
in Illinois, Wisconsin,
and Iowa

After Cleng Peerson opened the Midwest to Norwegian immigration, thousands of settlers migrated to Illinois, Wisconsin, and Iowa.

persuaded most of the settlers to move to Illinois. In 1834 and 1835, they left Kendall to establish the Fox River settlement.

By this time, a few immigrants were returning to Norway to visit their family and friends. A settler who had lived in both the Kendall and Fox River settlements, Knud Andersen Slogvig, returned to Norway in 1836. His excited accounts of the growth of the two settlements made others eager to join him on his trip back to the United States. Slogvig quickly organized a group of about 170, and they sailed from Stavanger that summer in the first emigration of its size.

The group went first to Rochester, New York, then traveled west to Illinois. A number stopped in Chicago, where they formed the beginning of the Norwegian settlement there, but the majority went to the Fox River colony, which by this time was a thriving settlement.

The years 1836 and 1837 marked the beginning of yearly emigration from Norway. In 1837 two shiploads of people —about 200 in all—left for America. For most of them, their first destination was Fox River.

Ole Rynning, whose book about America would influence so many Norwegians, intended to lead one of the groups to Fox River. When the group reached Chicago, however, speculators advised Rynning to go instead to the Beaver Creek region about 70 miles farther south. There, they said, he would find better land.

Rynning led the group to Beaver Creek, where they built log houses and spent the winter. But in the spring, the settlers learned the true character of the land—it was a swamp, teeming with mosquitoes. Malaria broke out. Many of the settlers died, including Rynning, who wrote his *True Account of America* as he lay ill. The following year, most of Beaver Creek's survivors moved to Fox River.

Ole Nattestad, one of the original settlers in Beaver Creek, left the settlement early to find better land. He traveled north and west, and when he settled to farm, he became the first Norwegian settler in Wisconsin. For a whole year, he was the only Norwegian settler in the area. But in September 1839, Ole's brother Ansten Nattestad brought a large group of emigrants from Norway to join Ole at his settlement. Called Jefferson Prairie, this settlement grew steadily and became a point of departure for settlers going farther west and north. Others from Nattestad's immigrant group settled at Rock Prairie, near Beloit, and this became another starting point for settlers moving west.

In 1839 immigrant leader John Nelson Luraas led a group of immigrants from New York, where they had just arrived, in the direction of Illinois. They stopped in Milwaukee, where a guide took them to the north end of Muskego Lake. The land looked inviting to the newcomers, for there was plenty of timber for houses and fuel. They bought the land and established the Muskego colony.

This was also a marshy area with poor soil, yet the Muskego settlement grew and spread into other counties until it was the most noted Norwegian settlement in Wisconsin. Many Norwegian-American religious, social, and cultural institutions began in the Muskego colony in the 1840s and 1850s.

Minister C. L. Clausen organized the first Norwegian Lutheran congregation and Sunday school in Muskego, and he built the first Norwegian Lutheran church in 1845. The first Norwegian-American newspaper was founded here in 1847—and called *Nordlyset* (Northern Lights)—by James D. Reymert, who had been a lawyer in Norway. So many newcomers stopped in Muskego on their way to the West that the settlement is considered the parent colony of many other Norwegian settlements in Wisconsin.

The number of Norse immigrants increased rapidly in the early 1840s, from 300 in 1840 to 1,660 in 1843. After 1843 the immigrants coming in one year never numbered fewer than 1,000. By the late 1840s, many ship captains were visiting Norway's inland valleys, villages, and towns to enroll emigrants. This became a profitable business for shipowners. American land agents also urged the people to come and settle, especially in the states of the Upper Midwest, where land was plentiful and fairly cheap. The prairie regions, however, did not attract the earliest settlers. From Fox River in Illinois, they preferred to move north to Wisconsin, where there

The first Norwegian-American Lutheran Church building was erected at the Muskego settlement in 1844-45. The building was used as a barn late in the century, and in 1904 it was dismantled and reconstructed at Luther Theological Seminary in St. Paul.

Hardanger costumes on display at Augsburg College in Minneapolis. The white dress in the center is a traditional Norwegian bridal gown from about 1905.

was more timber. They thought that where trees grew in abundance the soil had to be richer and more fertile than in the open prairie.

In the 1840s, Norwegians tended to settle the lands in southern and central Wisconsin. When those lands were taken, the movement began toward the west and northwest. By 1845 this movement had spread into northeastern Iowa, when settlers from Rock Prairie and Koshkonong in Wisconsin began to push in that direction.

Fewer Norwegians went to Iowa than to its neighboring states (in 1870 Wisconsin had 60,000 Norwegians and Iowa had about 25,000), but the Norwegians in Iowa were at least as culturally active as those in other Norwegian centers of population.

In 1861 Luther College was established in Decorah, Iowa. Several years later, the weekly newspaper *Decorah-Posten* was first issued. It was a popular Norwegian-language newspaper for 99 years, until it went out of publication in

1973. Vesterheim, Decorah's Norwegian-American museum, was founded in 1877. Its exhibits include a model of the *Restauration,* a log cabin, and Norwegian folk art. Decorah also holds an annual Nordic Fest—a celebration of traditional Norwegian foods, dancing, and music—that attracts vistors from all around the United States, as well as from Norway and Canada.

In the late 1840s, several Norwegian colonies were formed in Texas. Johan R. Reiersen led the first group in 1845; the largest and most important colony was founded in central Texas near Waco in 1853. None of these settlements grew rapidly, however, because during the Civil War years, the majority of Norwegian Americans sided with the North and were unwilling to move to the southern states. Not until 1890 did the Norwegian population in Texas exceed 1,000. Reiersen's dream of a large, compact colony that would attract thousands of oppressed and poor families from Norway was never realized. The major movements of Norwegians in America continued to be toward the north and west.

Carved spoons brought from Norway by immigrants in the 19th century

Minnesota

Newcomers to the Muskego colony often asked Reverend Clausen for advice about land. By 1850 the unsettled portions of southern Wisconsin were in the hands of land speculators and were too expensive

Retsius and Emma Nelson settled in northwestern Minnesota with their seven children.

for the immigrants. Reverend Clausen wanted to find out where cheaper land could be bought.

Minnesota had become a territory in 1849, and new land was being opened there. Reverend Clausen wrote to Governor Ramsey for information, and in the spring of 1850 Clausen visited St. Paul to investigate the possibility of acquiring land for a Norwegian settlement. His report to the newcomers in Wisconsin was favorable. Governor Ramsey was happy to welcome the Norwegians as settlers.

The first permanent settlements of Norse immigrants were in Goodhue County in southeastern Minnesota in 1851. Every year thereafter, families took a steamboat west across the Mississippi at La Crosse, Wisconsin, a departure point for immigrants moving into Minnesota. For many years, three counties in southeastern Minnesota —Fillmore, Houston, and Goodhue— attracted most of the settlers. In 10 years, 12,000 Norwegians settled in Minnesota, and more than half of them were in these counties. By 1870 there were 50,000 Norwegians in the state, and half of them lived in the three counties.

In 1862 the Homestead Act was passed by the United States Congress. A new immigrant could receive 160 acres (64 hectares) of government land free, for a promise to live on the land for five years and make improvements. At the end of that time, a settler had only to pay a small fee for the deed to the piece of land.

By this time, most of the land in the settled areas had been taken. What remained was in the hands of speculators and was, again, too expensive for newcomers. So a westward movement continued, this time along the Minnesota River Valley, where there was plenty of free government land. Though they still preferred the wooded areas, the settlers had discovered that the rolling prairie lands did contain rich, fertile soil. They also found that preparing the soil for growing crops there was much simpler and required less work than in the wooded areas.

When railroads were built in the 1870s, most of them extended west or northwest from St. Paul. Railroad companies were eager to promote settlements on the frontier and did much to encourage the immigrants to move in that direction. Soon the prairie lands and the wooded sections were settled, and still Norse immigrants came into the state. By 1900, about 800,000 Norwegian immigrants and

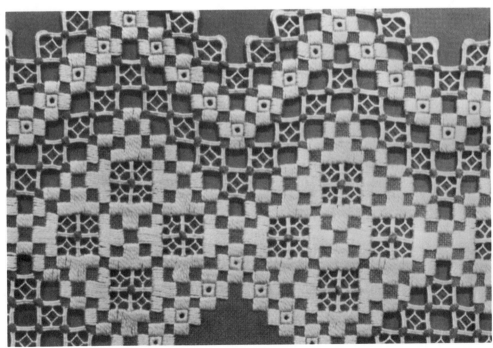

Many Norwegian immigrant women created fine embroidery.

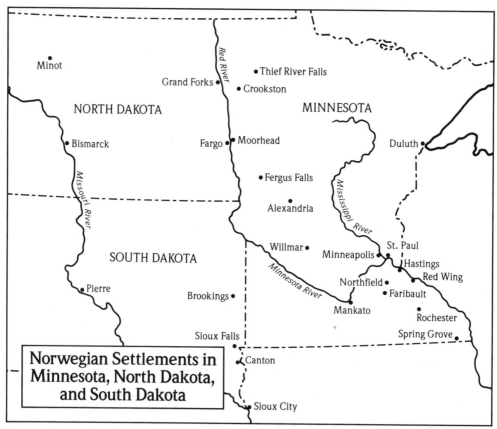

Norwegian settlers in Minnesota, North Dakota, and South Dakota moved north and west as they followed the Minnesota and Red rivers.

their children were living in the United States. One-third of this number lived in Minnesota. In fact, more Norwegians —first, second, and third generations— still live in Minnesota than in any other state.

Minnesota has three of the finest Norwegian-American colleges in the country—St. Olaf College, in Northfield, founded in 1874; Concordia College, in Moorhead, founded in 1891; and Augsburg College, in Minneapolis, which in 1922 grew out of Augsburg Seminary, founded in 1896.

The Red River Valley and the Dakotas

The opening of land for settlement in the Dakota Territory in 1861 marked the beginning of mass emigration from Norway. In 1882, the peak year, nearly 30,000 Norwegian immigrants entered the United States.

Paul Hjelm-Hansen, a Norwegian journalist who had criticized the church and state, became interested in the emigration movement because of his difficulties with state officials in Norway. In the middle 1860s, he was asked by the Minnesota Board of Immigration to explore the western part of the state, which the board was eager to have settled. He explored the Red River Valley for several weeks and declared it fertile land, free from stumps and stones, with clean air. His enthusiastic report was published as a series of articles in two widely circulated Norwegian-American newspapers—*Nordisk Folkeblad* (The Nordic People's Paper) and *Faedrelandet og Emigranten* (The Fatherland and the Emigrant)—and helped direct the flow of Norwegian settlers into western Minnesota and the Dakotas.

As the Norwegians moved into the area, they settled along the rivers, and especially along the Red River. Here they raised wheat and other grains and built towns, naming them after their homes in Norway—Halstad, Oslo, Veblen, and Hitterdal. The cities of Fargo and Grand Forks in North Dakota and Sioux Falls in South Dakota became trade and cultural centers for the Norwegian population in the Red River Valley. By 1880, more than 20,000 Norwegians had settled in the Dakota

Reidar Rosenvinge displays his rosemaling at the Norway Center in Chicago. Rosemaling thrived in rural Norway during the 18th and 19th centuries. The bygdelags, which inspired a greater appreciation for Norwegian folk art, kept the tradition alive in the United States.

Violinist Ole Bull

Territory, the majority in the eastern part. Twenty years later, in 1900, over 50,000 Norwegian Americans lived in South Dakota and 75,000 in North Dakota. At the time, North Dakota was the most Norwegian state, and until 1920, the Norwegians were North Dakota's largest ethnic group.

The Atlantic Coast

Although most lived in the Upper Midwest, many Norwegians settled along the Atlantic coast. Through the 1840s, most immigrants landed in New York, and a few sailors, carpenters, and other skilled workers from each immigrant group stayed on the East Coast to find work in their particular trades. Beginning in 1850, most immigrants landed in Quebec, but many skilled laborers traveled from here to New York. New York City's colony of skilled workers and professionals grew; by 1940 between 40,000 and 50,000 first- and second-generation Norwegians lived there.

Other small Norwegian settlements were formed in the New York cities of Troy, Albany, and Schenectady, where the Norwegians worked as engineers and machinists for the General Electric Company. At the turn of the century, a few expert glassblowers came from Norway to work at the Corning Glass Works. Later many other skilled glassblowers came until there was a colony of about 200 or 300 living in Corning, New York.

Another eastern colony was founded by Ole Bull, a world-famous Norwegian violinist, but it failed tragically. As Bull traveled throughout the United States on an extensive two-year concert tour in the 1840s, he learned about the Norwegian settlements in the Midwest. In 1852 he decided to establish an American colony for the poor people of Norway. To that end he bought, or thought that he bought, 120,000 acres (48,000 hectares) of land in northwestern Pennsylvania. He invited Norwegian immigrants to settle the land. From Bull's great wealth they would be paid wages for clearing land and building houses in a village named Oleana.

The first colonists arrived in September of 1852, and by year's end 250 people lived there. Many immigrants came to this colony with high hopes of obtaining new homes and a better

Sampling the buffet at Minnekirken, the Norwegian Memorial Lutheran Church in Chicago. The church is the only Norwegian-speaking congregation remaining in Chicago and one of just two in the country. (Another Norwegian-speaking congregation, also called Minnekirken, is located in Minneapolis.) This buffet is a part of the church's celebration of Syttende Mai.

Thousands of Norwegians found work in lumber mills on the Pacific Coast. By 1900, Scandinavians made up 25 percent of all forestry workers in the state of Washington.

life, only to find that Ole Bull had fallen victim to a group of swindlers. Those who sold him the land did not have clear title to it, and the situation cost Bull more money than even he could afford. In September 1853, Bull sold the land at a great loss, after most of Oleana's colonists had already moved on to other settlements farther west.

The Pacific Northwest

After the Dakotas were settled, Norwegians made a few settlements in Montana. Around 1900, pioneers moved to eastern Montana. Others excavated minerals in Idaho, western Montana, and eastern Colorado.

But the greatest number of Norwegian Americans who journeyed beyond the Dakotas went over the plains and mountains to the Pacific Northwest. The climate appealed to the farmers—no droughts, no blizzards, no scorching heat, and no swarms of grasshoppers, as they had found in the Upper Midwest. Other Norwegian immigrants were attracted by the fishing and lumber industries and settled in the Puget Sound region of Washington. Although Norwegians were not the founders of the fishing industry in the Pacific Northwest, many developed it into a major industry and a major source of livelihood for Norwegians living in the area.

As the 1990s began, Seattle had the greatest concentration of Norwegian businesses anywhere in the United States, with 30 Norwegian-owned companies. The *Western Viking* is a popular Norwegian-American newspaper that is still published. Seattle's Nordic Heritage Museum, founded in 1979, tells the story of Scandinavian immigrants in the Pacific Northwest and the merging of their traditions and customs with American culture.

Skøgfjorden Language Village, a Norwegian-language camp located near Bemidji, Minnesota, is sponsored by Concordia College at Moorhead, Minnesota.

After services at Minne-kirken, the Norwegian Memorial Lutheran Church in Minneapolis

A Norwegian-American Press

As the immigrants moved west, they saw their communities disperse. Most Norwegian Americans shared the tradition of the Lutheran church, but as early as the 1840s and 1850s they understood that they needed more to hold their growing population together. A Norwegian-language press seemed to be the answer. Not only could a newspaper educate those who were unable to read newspapers in English, but it would also improve communication between the scattered Norwegian-American settlements.

Nordlyset (Northern Lights) was the first Norwegian-immigrant newspaper, founded in Muskego in July of 1847. In

its pages, editor James D. Reymert printed the laws of Wisconsin, a message from Wisconsin's governor, and the inaugural address of President Zachary Taylor. The paper brought news from western settlements in Texas, Oregon, and California and from other distant places—including Norway. Two hundred people eventually subscribed to *Nordlyset,* at a price of $2 per year. This wasn't enough to support the paper, however, and it folded in its second year.

Emigranten, founded in January 1852, became the first major pioneer newspaper. Muskego minister C.L. Clausen was its first editor, when the paper first declared itself a voice for the Democratic party. When Carl Fredrik Solberg became the editor in 1857, he moved *Emigranten* into the Republican camp, and the circulation dramatically increased. Norwegian Americans had traditionally supported Democratic ideals, but the Republican party began to represent Protestantism and prohibition, two important causes to Norwegian-American voters.

An effort to stop this apparent change in political course produced several new Norwegian newspapers.

Like the first paper, *Nordlyset,* later papers contained news reports, speeches, documents, editorials, and controversial essays. Some newspapers included news of social events

When the Decorah-Posten stopped publication in 1973, it was the last Norwegian-American paper in the Midwest.

and gave advice and hints for daily life in the United States. A few Norwegian immigrant newspapers even printed modern Norwegian literature, in serial installments. It was a special purpose of the immigrant press to maintain contact with life in Norway.

Hundreds of Norwegian-American newspapers eventually developed, though most were short-lived. Three Midwestern newspapers became very successful as the country's expanding railroads brought them to the most distant regions of Norwegian settlement.

Skandinaven (1866–1941), published in Chicago, reached a high point in 1912 with almost 54,000 subscribers to its semi-weekly edition. A daily edition had a circulation of 25,000. The paper was popular in tone and sympathetic to the Haugean lay movement occurring in the Lutheran church.

Decorah-Posten (1874–1973) kept distant from political and religious controversy; its position was merely to report facts. It was also the only immigrant newspaper to have a comic strip. In the 1920s, the weekly paper reached a high of about 45,000 subscribers.

By 1910 *Minneapolis Tidende* (1887–1935) had attained a circulation of nearly 33,000 for its weekly edition. The paper was also neutral in church and political affairs, and it gained recognition for its reviews of music and literature and for its attention to Norwegian cultural and social life.

Cultural Identity

At the time that the press was just beginning, people within the Norwegian-American community predicted that their culture would be quickly absorbed into the larger American culture. Norwegian Americans readily learned to speak English, and they were well accepted by their non-Norwegian neighbors.

The Norwegian Americans retained their ethnic identity for many more decades, however, for several reasons. One was the Norwegian-American press that worked to unite its readership. Another was the continuing stream of immigrants that came into the United States until World War I began, reinforcing each community's ties to Norway. Yet another reason was the emergence of Norway as a fully independent nation in 1905. The event was headline news in the United States; America "discovered" Norway. Norwegian Americans basked in the approval of their fellow citizens and gained respect for their own heritage. They were very proud to be Norwegian.

The number of Norwegian-American cultural organizations rapidly increased during the period from 1895 to the beginning of World War I (1914). The first Sons of Norway lodge was founded in Minneapolis in 1895. Within 20 years, the Sons of Norway had 135 lodges and a membership of 12,000. What started as a mutual aid fund later

Sweden recognized Norway's independence in 1905, and in 1906, Prince Carl of Denmark was crowned king of Norway. He took the name Haakon VII, thereby continuing the line of Norwegian kings that had ended with the death of King Haakon VI in 1380.

became a large insurance company that also published a monthly periodical and sponsored a wide range of cultural events. The Norwegian Society of America was founded in 1903, with a goal of uniting all Norwegian Americans around the cause of Norwegian language, literature, and immigrant history.

Bygdelags

The Norwegian immigrants often came in groups from a particular Norwegian *bygd,* or district, and they settled together in the United States. One group from Norway's Numedal district, for example, settled at Jefferson Prairie, while another settled at eastern Koshkonong. Many Stavanger people went to Fox River. Muskego attracted those from Telemark. A Vossing group settled in Chicago, and a Hallingdal group at Rock Prairie. A large settlement often was home to people from several *bygds,* but *bygd* groups were clearly defined within the community.

This immigrant need for the familiar eventually gave rise to the *bygdelag* (district society) movement, which officially began in 1902 when the first

A Sons of Norway **lutefisk** *dinner. Lutefisk, or dried cod, is a popular dish among Norwegian Americans.*

bygdelag was formed. The explicit goal of the *bygdelag* was the preservation of the distinctive markings of a culture, for life in one Norwegian *bygd* could vary greatly from that of another. Variations among cultures in Norway were due to the country's geography and terrain, which divided people by mountains and fjords (inlets of the sea). Each *bygd* had its own songs, folk tales, and customs, as well as distinctive styles of dress, artistic expression, and humor. The most obvious distinguishing characteristic of the *bygd*, however, was its dialect, or variety of speech. Within two decades, nearly 50 societies came into being, and at least 75,000 people took part in the reunions each year.

A *bygdelag* reunion, called a *stevne*, was a 2- or 3-day event of celebrating and socializing that was like a visit to the group's homeland. The reunions were the only place where rural Norwegian dialects were fully accepted outside the home. For this reason, the *bygdelags* were especially popular with those in agricultural communities of the United States and those who cherished their rural pasts. *Bygdelag* members felt they needed to assert themselves against what they perceived as city arrogance and against the people who worked toward a refined Norwegian culture. People in the cities, on the other hand, feared that the rural tradition would have too much influence in the shaping of a Norwegian-American culture. They did

Mr. Jørgen Hyland, at home in Evanston, Illinois, plays a Hardanger fiddle.

not want to reinforce the already-widespread view of Norwegians as "country folk," or peasants. The growth of the *bygdelags* was therefore accompanied by strong tensions.

Americans

Bygdelags and other Norwegian-American cultural societies became a force that worked to maintain an ethnic identity. A vast majority of Norwegian Americans did not participate in any ethnic activity, however. In 1899,

membership of all Norwegian-American cultural societies was approximately 15,000. In 1914, it was about 60,000. Although the fourfold increase is significant, 60,000 was still a relatively small minority of a population that by 1910 was 1,500,000.

Norwegian culture was merging with the American culture at large, and there was visible change even in the Norwegian Americans' strongest institution—the church. When the Norwegian Lutheran Church in America was born in 1917, with the uniting of the three major Norwegian church

Vinland National Center, with facilities on Lake Independence in Minnesota, is a rehabilitation agency for people with special challenges and disabilities. A nonprofit organization, it started with funds from Norway's royal family in 1976. Vinland's services include vocational rehabilitation and chemical-dependency treatment. It serves more than 3,000 people annually.

synods—the Norwegian Synod, the Haugean Synod, and the United Norwegian Lutheran Church—the Americanization of the Lutheran church proceeded rapidly. The church began to change over to the English language, in order to minister to an English-speaking generation. Toward the end of World War II, fewer than 7 percent of all services in the Lutheran churches were conducted in Norwegian. The Norwegian Lutheran Church in America dropped the word "Norwegian" from its name in 1946. In 1960, it united with German and Danish Lutheran groups.

Norwegians were also merging into the American work force. By 1925 the distribution of Norwegians in the specialized professions was proportionate to their share of the American population. Most showed a strong preference for farming and fishing, but many Norwegian-American men were also engineers, architects, pastors, and lawyers. At first women worked mainly in domestic occupations, if they worked outside their homes at all, but gradually they became well represented in other fields. Many worked in telephone and telegraph companies; others were clerical workers, teachers, and nurses.

Many second- and third-generation Norwegian Americans still operate farms, like this dairy farm in Wisconsin.

4
CONTRIBUTIONS TO AMERICAN LIFE

So many Norwegian immigrants to Wisconsin started tobacco farms that the crop was soon known as a Norwegian-American specialty in that state.

Agriculture

The Norwegians' move from rural farm life in Norway to a similar lifestyle in America could be considered a conservative change. But Norwegian immigrant farmers made many adjustments that called for adaptability and inventiveness as they learned about new crops and new farming methods. The Norwegians quickly began cultivating tobacco, for example, a crop that was unfamiliar to them in Norway.

Some Norwegian Americans became inventors and producers of farm machinery. Targe G. Mandt from Telemark, Norway, was a blacksmith who had worked during the Civil War in a Missouri factory that built wagons for the Union Army. In 1865, Mandt went to Stoughton, Wisconsin, where he started his own factory with only $40. His wagons, ploughs, and farm implements were soon used by farmers throughout the Upper Midwest. The Gisholt Manufacturing Company of Madison, Wisconsin, also became a large producer of farm machinery. Its founder, John Anders Johnson, who had come from Norway in the 1840s, invented a turret lathe that was sold all over the world.

The most noted agriculturalist of Norwegian descent is scientist Norman Borlaug. Borlaug, whose parents were immigrants from Norway, was born in 1914 and grew up on a farm in Cresco, Iowa. He studied forestry and plant pathology at the University of Minnesota and then worked for several years as a biochemist with E.I. du Pont de Nemours & Company. In 1944, Borlaug joined a team of scientists to study farming problems in Mexico, out of which the International Maize and Wheat Improvement Center was born.

Farmers in Mexico grew a variety of wheat with very long stems. The heavy heads of wheat would bend the thin stems, making crops difficult to harvest. To solve the problem, Borlaug's group developed a new variety of wheat, drawing on a type of short-stemmed wheat grown in Japan. The group achieved similar success developing new, high-yielding varieties of rice and corn. This progress led to a phenomenon known as the "Green Revolution," the great increase in grain production during the 1960s that led many people to believe world hunger could be solved. Borlaug was highly sought as a consultant to countries struggling with low crop yields. In this capacity, he traveled to India, Pakistan, Afghanistan, Tunisia, and Morocco. In 1970 Norman Borlaug was awarded the Nobel Peace Prize for his work with wheat.

Norman Borlaug

Business and Industry

Norwegian Americans in business fields are relatively few, but several have enjoyed great success. One such person was Arthur Andersen (1885–1947). In 1913, when income-tax legislation was being passed by the U.S. Congress, Andersen and several partners organized an accounting firm to handle tax problems. By 1990 Arthur Andersen's offices had reached every

Earl Bakken

spent a brief period in politics as an elected member of New Mexico's first state legislature, which convened in 1912. He also tried a career in banking. Starting out as a cashier of a San Antonio bank, he was president of the same bank within two years. Shortly after serving in World War I, Hilton bought his first hotel. He proved to be a master of financing as he continued to purchase large, established hotels, such as the Palmer House in Chicago and the Waldorf-Astoria in New York City. The Hilton Hotel Corporation, managed since 1966 by Conrad's son Barron Hilton, now has hotels in all the major cities of the world.

As the founder of Medtronic, Incorporated, Earl Bakken is known for more than his entrepreneurial spirit; he is also credited with giving new life to thousands of heart patients. When Bakken started the company with his brother-in-law, Palmer Hermundslie, he gained a solid reputation designing customized medical equipment. And when heart surgeon Dr. C. Walton Lillehei needed an improved pacemaker for his infant patients, he asked Bakken to take on the job. Bakken designed a battery-operated model that was far superior to the electrical type common at the time. He then teamed up with another pair of inventors to produce the first successful implantable pacemaker with its own power supply. Medtronic has manufactured this pacemaker worldwide and has sold them in 75 countries.

major city in the United States and 54 foreign countries, to rank as the third largest accounting firm in the world. Acting on his interest in education and Norwegian cultural traditions, Andersen was a benefactor of St. Olaf College and Luther College and was president of the Norwegian-American Historical Association from 1936 to 1942.

Conrad Hilton (1914–1979), the man who became known internationally as the Hotel King, grew up in New Mexico. During his youth, Hilton assisted his Norwegian immigrant father with his many businesses and eventually became a full business partner. Hilton

The Lincoln Tunnel, the world's only three-tube vehicular tunnel, provides a vital link under the Hudson River between midtown Manhattan and Weehawken, New Jersey. It was built by Norwegian immigrant Ole Singstad.

Engineering and Science

As American cities grew, they demanded new roads, tunnels, bridges, and skyscrapers, causing the job market in transportation and construction to expand rapidly. Technically educated Norwegians were among those attracted to America for its employment opportunities.

Ole Singstad (1882–1969), born and educated in Norway as a civil engineer, worked on many of the tunnels connecting America's first highways. He came to the United States in 1905, and by 1920 he was working for a man named Clifford M. Holland, who had been hired to design an underwater tunnel that would connect Manhattan, New York, and Jersey City, New Jersey. Singstad, Holland, and Holland's assistant, Milton H. Freeman, overcame extremely difficult river-bottom conditions to build the tunnel, which also contained an advanced ventilating system. When Holland died in 1924 and Freeman died the following year, Singstad carried the Holland Tunnel to its completion. Singstad was also the consulting engineer for the Posey Tube —the tunnel connecting Oakland and Alameda in California. He built the Lincoln and Queens Midtown tunnels in New York City and many other tunnels in New York, Boston, Baltimore, and Detroit. When Singstad retired in 1945, he was recognized as the greatest tunnel authority in the world.

Dozens of magnificent federal and municipal buildings in the United States were designed and constructed by business partners Gunvald Aus (an engineer) and Kort Berle (an architect). In the 20 years of their partnership, they built the post offices and court-houses in Denver, Cleveland, New Orleans, Providence, and New Haven. They also built the Supreme Court building in Washington, D.C., and the U.S. Customs House in New York City. But the skyscraper was their specialty, and New York's Woolworth Building, 60 stories high, is remembered as one of their greatest achievements.

Norwegian Americans have made important contributions to science, as demonstrated by the work of Dr. Ernest O. Lawrence and Dr. Conrad Elvehjem. As a physics professor at the University of California at Berkeley, Lawrence (1901–1951) researched the structure of the atom and the use of radiation in biology and medicine. He became world famous at the age of 30, when he invented the cyclotron—a powerful "gun" for smashing atoms and for bringing atomic particles to high speeds. The cyclotron made the release of atomic energy possible for the first time on a practical scale. It also produced the first uranium 235 and the first plutonium, both used as fuels for nuclear explosives. Scientists use the cyclotron for a variety of purposes, including medical research.

Lawrence received the 1939 Nobel Prize in physics for his invention and

One of the first American skyscrapers, the Woolworth Building in New York City brought acclaim to its creators, Kort Berle and Gunvald Aus.

development of the cyclotron. Also credited to Lawrence, but much less heralded, is the invention of another common device—the color television tube.

Dr. Conrad Elvehjem, a biochemist at the University of Wisconsin, made a very important discovery in 1937. He cured dogs of a sickness called black tongue by feeding them nicotinic acid. The acid was soon found to be effective in treating a similar sickness in humans, called pellagra, and the acid was added to the list of known vitamins under the name niacin, or vitamin B_6. Elvehjem's study led to the discovery that vitamin B, believed to contain only one vitamin, actually has at least six different elements, each with specific properties. Dr. Elvehjem later became dean of the graduate school and president of the university.

Knute Nelson

Government

A familiarity with democratic principles and local government in Norway encouraged many Norwegian Americans to participate in U.S. government. Many of them served on agricultural committees and were dedicated to improving the farm economies of the areas they represented.

Wisconsin, Minnesota, Iowa, and the Dakotas have elected many Norwegian Americans to the U.S. Congress. Knute Nelson of Minnesota was the first

Norwegian to serve in Congress. Born in Norway in 1843, Nelson came to the United States in 1849 and grew up on a Wisconsin farm. In 1883 he was elected to the U.S. House of Representatives, and in 1892 he was elected governor of Minnesota. He resigned in 1895 to serve in the United States Senate, where he remained for 28 years until his death in 1923. A moderate Republican, Nelson supported such measures as a lower tax on imported goods, antitrust and income-tax legislation, and United States membership in the League of Nations.

held the record for longest continuous service in Congress (34 years). He was born in Wisconsin to immigrant parents, and he farmed for many years before entering politics. While serving in the U.S. House of Representatives, he acted as chair of the House Committee on Agriculture.

Few Norwegian-American women have served in Congress. Coya Knutson, however, was a very popular congressional representative in the 1950s. She was born Cornelia Gjesdal to Norwegian immigrant parents in North Dakota. After she married and moved to Oklee, Minnesota, she farmed for years with her husband, taught school, and managed a hotel in the small town. Inspired by First Lady Eleanor Roosevelt, Knutson then decided to enter politics, and in November 1950, she won a seat in the Minnesota legislature. In 1954 Knutson became the first woman from Minnesota elected to the U.S. Congress. When she was appointed to the House Committee on Agriculture, she achieved another first—no other woman had ever received this appointment.

Improving Minnesota's farm economy was Knutson's top priority. She also wrote and supported bills to aid Native American peoples and to provide research money for cystic fibrosis. She wrote a college student-loan bill

Another member of U.S. Congress from Minnesota was Andrew Volstead (1860–1947), who is chiefly remembered for the Prohibition Act, which he introduced in 1919. This legislation was passed by Congress over the veto of President Woodrow Wilson and became known as the Volstead Act. It provided for enforcement of the 18th Amendment to the U.S. Constitution, which forbade the national manufacture, sale, transportation, and use of intoxicating liquors. When the amendment was repealed in 1933, the Volstead Act died with it.

Gilbert Haugen (1859–1933), a Republican representing Iowa, once

Hubert H. Humphrey and his wife, Muriel, visiting the birthplace of Humphrey's mother in Kristiansand, Norway

that was modeled after legislation passed years earlier in Norway. Knutson served until 1958, and she went on to work as congressional liaison to the Pentagon's Office of Civil Defense, where she worked for 10 years.

Two Norwegian Americans, Hubert H. Humphrey and Walter F. Mondale, have served as vice president of the United States. Humphrey, born in South Dakota in 1911, began his political career as Minnesota's state campaign director for Franklin D. Roosevelt during the 1944 presidential campaign. Humphrey attracted much attention that year as he helped merge the Democratic and Farmer-Labor parties in the state, and in 1945 he was elected mayor of Minneapolis. In 1948 Humphrey was elected to the United States Senate, where he served for three terms before becoming vice president under Lyndon Johnson in 1964. Humphrey became the Democratic party's candidate for president in the summer of 1968, but Richard Nixon, the Republican candidate, defeated him by a narrow margin that November. In 1970 Humphrey returned to the Senate and served until his death in 1978. Known as a liberal, Humphrey was elected by his fellow senators to the position of assistant majority leader in 1961, and in 1964 he guided the passage of civil-rights legislation.

Walter F. Mondale took the seat vacated by Hubert Humphrey in 1964, and he represented Minnesota in the U.S. Senate for 12 years. He then served as vice president under Jimmy Carter until 1980. The Carter-Mondale ticket was defeated in its 1980 reelection bid, and Mondale ran unsuccessfully for president in 1984. He then returned to a career in law.

Mondale has credited his progressive political thinking to his Norwegian heritage. Concern for quality education, good health care, and economic policies that provide jobs are democratic traditions that have long been a part of daily life in Norway.

Another Norwegian American who achieved national prominence was Earl Warren (1891–1974). With a background in California politics, including 10 years as governor of the state, Warren was named chief justice of the Supreme Court by President Dwight

Walter Mondale campaigning with his vice presidential running mate, Geraldine Ferraro, in 1984. Ferraro was the first woman to be nominated for the office of vice president of the United States.

Floyd B. Olson

Eisenhower. During Warren's service, the Court made a landmark ruling on school segregation, stating that separate schools were "inherently unequal." This ruling, which Warren made early in his career as Chief Justice, established his presence on the Supreme Court as a liberal and influential leader. Warren also served as chair of the presidential commission that investigated the assassination of President John F. Kennedy. A popular leader, Warren suffered only one political defeat during his career—when he ran for U.S. vice president on Thomas Dewey's ticket in 1948 and lost.

Many Norwegian Americans have been elected to the office of governor, particularly in the state of Minnesota. Floyd B. Olson (1891–1936) was first elected governor of Minnesota in 1930, and he served until his death in 1936. His strong leadership during the Depression made him very popular, because he worked hard for passage of unemployment and farm relief legislation and supported labor during the strikes of the time. Karl Rolvaag (1913–1990) was Minnesota's governor from 1963 to 1967. The son of author Ole E. Rolvaag, Karl was appointed ambassador to Iceland during the administration of President Lyndon Johnson. Albert H. Quie, born in 1923, became the governor of Minnesota in 1980 after serving in the U.S. House of Representatives for 22 years. While in Congress, Quie was a leading advocate of agricultural reform and a senior member of the House Committee on Agriculture.

Martin Sabo is a Minnesota member of the U.S. House of Representatives. He was born in North Dakota in 1938, and he was educated at Augsburg College in Minneapolis. At age 22 he won a seat in the Minnesota House of Representatives and was the youngest legislator in the nation at that time. He served until 1978, when he was elected to the U.S. House. In 1990 Sabo was elected to a fourth term.

Martin Sabo

Medicine

Very few doctors came with the first wave of 19th-century Norwegian immigration. Later, when the technically educated began arriving from Norway's cities, more doctors came to the United States. Prominent Norwegian American physicians of the 19th and 20th centuries have done significant work, particularly in heart surgery and cancer research.

Dr. Ludwig Hektoen (1863–1951), born in Wisconsin of Norse immigrant parents, was a noted pathologist who specialized in coronary thrombosis and cancer research and was among the few internationally known researchers who studied treatments for amoebic dysentery. Outstanding among his achievements, however, was his work with blood transfusions, and Dr. Hektoen is credited as the first to match blood types of donors and recipients. He was affiliated with many hospitals and research centers, most notably the University of Chicago, where from 1901 to 1932 he served as professor and head of the Department of Pathology. He served as president of the Chicago Tumor Institute from 1938 until his death.

Alfred Owre (1870–1935) came to Minneapolis from Norway with his parents. He received his degree from the University of Minnesota School of Dentistry in 1894 and became dean of the school in 1905. Owre believed that dentistry should be closely integrated with medicine; he suspected that tooth decay and oral diseases were caused in part by poor nutrition and by diseases affecting other parts of the body. He traveled to Russia, Germany, and Austria to study the relationship of the dental and medical professions in those countries, and when he returned to Minnesota he campaigned to unite American dentistry and medicine. In 1927 he became dean of the School of Dental and Oral Surgery at Columbia University, where he remained until 1935.

Chest specialist Dr. Owen Wangensteen (1898–1981) received his education in the United States and Europe. He was director of surgery and chief surgeon at the University of Minnesota hospitals from 1926 until his retirement in 1967. Dr. C. Walton Lillehei was also a distinguished surgeon who pioneered in open-heart surgery during the 1950s and 1960s. He did important work with infants suffering from congenital heart conditions, and he significantly increased their survival rates. Dr. Lillehei held positions on the staffs of the University of Minnesota Medical School and the Cornell University Medical Center.

Two Norwegian-American cancer researchers to work into the 1990s are Leon Orris Jacobson of Chicago and Dr. Haakon Ragde of Seattle. At the University of Chicago, Dr. Jacobson developed methods to study the after-effects of nuclear test bombing and studied the biological effects of war gases that mimic the effects of radiation. Some of his testing has resulted in effective treatment of Hodgkin's disease. Dr. Ragde is a prominent urological surgeon who was born in Norway. He is credited with bringing to the United States a Danish-developed ultrasonic method for the early detection of prostate cancer.

Education and Scholarship

Because many Norwegian immigrants came from rural communities in Norway where public schools were not available, the ability to read and write was not universal among the immigrants. Of the Norwegians who emigrated before 1860, about 50 percent were literate. Norwegian Americans founded some of the United States' best colleges, however, and many first- and second-generation Norwegian Americans became outstanding scholars.

Thorstein Veblen (1857–1929) came from a large family of Norwegian immigrants who settled in Northfield, Minnesota. Educated at Carleton College, Johns Hopkins University, and

Agnes Wergeland was the first Norwegian woman in the world to receive a Ph.D. degree.

became head of the history department at the University of Wyoming. She is chiefly noted for her efforts to promote professional education for women.

The librarian who founded the Library of Congress cataloging system was James Christian Meinich Hanson (1864–1943). He was born in Norway and was educated in the United States. Hanson also reorganized the large library at the University of Chicago and cataloged the Vatican Library.

Two brothers, Theodore and Carl Blegen, contributed to scholarship in the fields of history and archaeology,

Yale University, Veblen became a noted economist, philosopher, social critic, and writer. His main work, *The Theory of the Leisure Class* (1899), made "conspicuous consumption" a catchphrase while attacking Americans' tendency toward materialism. A controversial figure, he has been called "the spiritual father of the New Deal."

Agnes Wergeland (1857–1914), born and educated in Norway, came to the United States as a lecturer in art history. She taught at Bryn Mawr and at the University of Chicago, and in 1902

Carl Blegen

respectively. Dr. Theodore Blegen (1891–1969), a history professor and dean of the Graduate School at the University of Minnesota, was a leading authority on Norwegian immigration to the United States. He wrote many volumes on this subject, and he translated into English many of the letters written by immigrants to their relatives in Norway.

Dr. Carl Blegen (1887–1971) was a professor of classical archaeology at the University of Cincinnati and was head of the Department of Classics for 30 years. From 1948 to 1949, he directed the American School of Classical Studies in Athens. He wrote several volumes about his excavations at the ancient city of Troy, where he found the remains of nine successive cities dating from 3000 B.C. to A.D. 300. In his later years, he directed archaeological work at Pylos in southwestern Greece.

Dr. Howard Hong, born in 1912, and his wife, Edna Hatlestad Hong, born in 1913, are the leading translators and interpreters of the works of Søren Kierkegaard, a Danish philosopher and religious thinker. Dr. and Mrs. Hong have devoted their lives to compiling, editing, and translating Kierkegaard's work into English. They won the National Book Award in 1968 for their work on the first of a seven-volume edition of Kierkegaard's journals and papers. Their 6,500-volume Kierkegaard library is housed at St. Olaf College in Northfield, Minnesota.

Einar Haugen is a leading scholar of Nordic languages. His studies of bilingualism and his work among Norwegian immigrants brought him international fame. He was born in Sioux City, Iowa, the son of Norwegian immigrants. While still a child, he moved with his parents to Norway, where they lived for two years before returning to the United States. He was a professor of Scandinavian languages and linguistics at Harvard University and has written a Norwegian-English dictionary and textbooks for students of the Norwegian language.

Einar Haugen

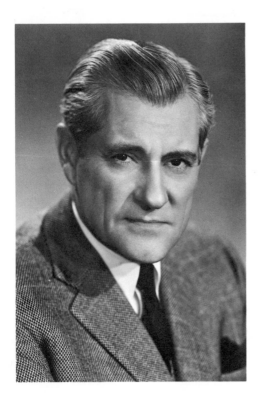

Journalism

In the first part of the 20th century, the United States had a flourishing pioneer press that included over 400 Norwegian-American newspapers. Countless distinguished journalists came from this tradition.

Victor F. Lawson (1850–1925) was the son of Ivar Lawson, who founded the *Skandinaven* with John Anderson in 1866. Victor continued the business after his father's death, and in 1876 he bought the *Chicago Daily News,* which had been founded by an old school friend, Melville E. Stone. The paper

was financially unstable and Stone needed to sell. As the new owner, editor-in-chief Lawson kept Stone on as an editor, and together the two made the *Daily News* one of the most respected papers in the country.

Lawson believed that a newspaper should be "candid, comprehensive, concise, clean, and cheap." A journalist of high ideals, Lawson also believed that reform was needed in the news-gathering process. In 1890 he was appointed to head a committee to investigate an alleged scandal in the United Press (a news-gathering service unrelated to United Press International). Rumors were circulating that a clique of financiers controlled the United Press, and that the United Press was pirating news stories from Associated Press reports. Lawson confirmed the rumors and exposed the scandal. He then set to work to unite the factions of the Associated Press and served as the first president of the new AP.

Lawson was a generous man. In 1866 he established a sanatorium for sick children in Chicago's tenement districts, and in his will he bequeathed large sums of money for civic improvement in Chicago.

Perhaps the most widely known journalist of Norwegian heritage is Eric Sevareid. Born in North Dakota in 1912, Sevareid received his education at the University of Minnesota. He worked for the *Minneapolis Journal* for a few years and then wrote for the Paris edition of the *New York Herald Tribune.* In 1939 he joined the Columbia Broadcasting System as a European correspondent, and during World War II he broadcast news from France, England, Holland, and Belgium. He then worked as a news commentator for CBS until his retirement in 1977.

Brenda Ueland (1891–1985) grew up in Minneapolis, the daughter of Andreas Ueland, a judge, and Clara Hampson Ueland, a human-rights activist who campaigned for prison reform, women's rights, and child-labor laws. Brenda Ueland was a journalist who wrote for both magazines and newspapers. In 1913 she became the first woman reporter to work for the *Minneapolis Tribune,* and in 1914 she worked briefly for the *St. Paul Daily News.* During the next decade, she lived in New York and Connecticut. While living on the East Coast, she wrote articles for dozens of magazines and was a member of the social set that included writers Eugene O'Neill, John Reed, and Louise Bryant. Ueland returned to Minneapolis in 1930, continuing her freelance career and working as a columnist at the *Minneapolis Times* from 1941 to 1948.

Ueland's grandson, Eric Utne, is also a journalist who became a publisher as well. A native of St. Paul, Minnesota, Utne first worked as an advertising director for *East West Journal,* then

Brenda Ueland

Publisher and editor Eric Utne is a founding member of the Social Venture Network, a national association of business people committed to social change.

Literature

The first Norwegian Americans had been in the United States for nearly 50 years before any of them published a novel or short story. But a Norwegian-American literature did finally emerge, intended chiefly to preserve Norwegian culture in America.

Ole E. Rolvaag (1876–1931) was an outstanding immigrant writer. He was born on the Norwegian island of Donna, where fishing was the only means of livelihood. At the age of 20, he immigrated to the United States and worked on an uncle's farm in South Dakota for several years. He attended Augustana Academy in Canton, South Dakota, and graduated from St. Olaf College in 1905. After a year of study at the University of Oslo, he returned to St. Olaf College as a professor of Norwegian language and literature, and he remained on the faculty until his death.

Although he is considered an American author, Rolvaag wrote in Norwegian and had his novels translated into English. He was a keen observer of immigrant life in the United States and a strong supporter of the idea that Norway's language, customs, and religion should be preserved in American life. In 1925 Rolvaag was one of the founders of the Norwegian-American Historical Association, established for the purpose of preserving Norwegian traditions. His first novel to be published in the United

helped start the *New Age Journal* in 1974. He worked for a time as a literary agent in New York City, then returned to Minneapolis, where he started a publication called the *Utne Reader* in 1984. What began as a newsletter soon grew into a magazine whose 1990 circulation topped 200,000. Called an alternative journal, the bimonthly magazine publishes articles that editor-in-chief Utne and his staff consider to be the best of America's growing fringe press.

States, *Giants in the Earth,* is an epic of immigrant life on the South Dakota prairie and is considered to be a masterpiece of American literature.

Writer and illustrator Ingri Parin d'Aulaire (1904–1980) was born in Norway and came to the United States in 1929. She and her Swiss husband, Edgar Parin d'Aulaire, collaborated for over 40 years on writing and illustrating children's books. In 1940 the d'Aulaires won the Caldecott Medal for their book *Abraham Lincoln.* Among their other works are *Children of the Northlights, Book of Greek Myths, Pocahontas, Buffalo Bill,* and *The Magic Meadow.*

Wallace Stegner, born in Iowa in 1909 to Norwegian immigrant parents, is a historian, biographer, and essayist. Dedicated to conservation, Stegner served as assistant secretary of the interior in 1961 and was a member of the National Parks Advisory Board in 1962. He spent four years teaching at Harvard, then taught English at Stanford University and directed Stanford's creative writing program from 1946 to 1971. He has written over 30 books, including *Angle of Repose,* which was awarded the Pulitzer Prize in fiction in 1972, and *The Spectator Bird,* which won the National Book Award in 1977.

Poet and translator Robert Bly was born in Madison, Minnesota, to Norwegian-American parents. He attended St. Olaf College, Harvard University, and the University of Iowa before studying in Norway from 1956 to 1957 on a Fulbright scholarship. While abroad he learned the Norwegian language and began to translate contemporary Norwegian poetry into English. When he returned to Minnesota, he settled on farmland that his father had given to him, and he farmed and continued translating. In 1957 Bly and his associate William Duffy began to publish a literary journal called *The Fifties.* In the next decade *The Fifties* became *The Sixties* (it has since been named *The Seventies, The Eighties,* and *The Nineties*), and Bly and Duffy

Wallace Stegner

Robert Bly

began publishing books of poetry. Bly's own books of poetry include *Silence in the Snowy Fields, The Light Around the Body* (which won the National Book Award for poetry in 1968), and *The Man in the Dark Coat Turns.* Bly is sometimes called the father of a school of literature known as "Deep Imagism" or "the New Surrealism" that tries to break the barrier between the conscious and the unconscious mind through use of images. Bly's nonfiction work *Iron John: A Book About Men* was published in 1990 and became a best-seller.

Music

Congregational singing has always been a strong tradition in the Lutheran church, and a popular musical form to come from Norway is the men's choir. Many Norwegian-American choral societies have been formed to promote singing, and large song festivals are a part of Scandinavian tradition that Norwegian Americans still enjoy.

The most noted Norwegian-American college choir is at St. Olaf College in Northfield, Minnesota. This choir was started by F. Melius Christiansen (1871–1955), who came to the United States in 1889 and served as director of the School of Music at St. Olaf College from 1903 to 1943. In addition to reviving the traditional music of Norway, one of Christiansen's ambitions was to introduce a cappella singing—singing without instrumental accompaniment—which at the time had not been attempted in America. He chose students with reedlike singing voices for his choir and trained them for a perfect blending of voices. Under his leadership, the choir became internationally known through tours of Europe and the United States. Dr. Christiansen was also a composer, and he arranged old Norse folk melodies, hymns, and chorales. His son Olaf followed him as director of the St. Olaf Choir, and another son, Paul, became director of the choir at Concordia College in Moorhead, Minnesota.

Conductor Ole Windingstad (1886–1959) was born in Norway and came to the United States after studying music in Oslo and Leipzig. Noted for introducing Scandinavian composers to American audiences, he was conductor of the Scandinavian Symphony Orchestra, the Brooklyn Symphony Orchestra, the Albany Symphony, and the New Orleans Symphony.

F. Melius Christiansen

Rise Stevens

Opera singer Rise Stevens was born in New York in 1913 and studied at the Juilliard School. A mezzo-soprano, she made her Metropolitan Opera debut in 1938 as Mignon, in Ambroise Thomas's opera of the same name. Stevens sang 23 consecutive seasons with the Met, during which she sang 220 performances of 15 different roles. She is best remembered for her Carmen, a role she sang 75 times on the Met's stage, and Octavian, from the opera *The Cavalier of the Rose* by Richard Strauss, a role she sang 50 times. Stevens also made several films, including *Going My Way* with Bing Crosby. After she served as director of the Metropolitan Opera National Company from 1965 to 1967 and as president of the Mannes College of Music in New York City from 1975 to 1978, Rise Stevens became an advisor to the Metropolitan Opera's young artist development program.

Entertainment and Sports

Few people of Norwegian extraction have entered the entertainment industry, but there are notable exceptions to the rule. James Arness, best known for his role as Marshal Matt Dillon in the television western "Gunsmoke," was from a Norwegian-American family. He starred in the show for 20 years. His brother Peter Graves was also a television actor who starred in the drama "Mission: Impossible" from 1967 to 1973.

Actor James Cagney (1899–1986) was of Norwegian descent. Born in New York City, he worked as a dancer in vaudeville for several years before becoming a screen actor. With *Public Enemy* in 1931, Cagney became an overnight success. While he won an Academy Award for his portrayal of the composer George M. Cohan in the film biography *Yankee Doodle Dandy*, Cagney was best known for his gangster roles, in great films such as *Angels with Dirty Faces* and *What Price Glory?*

James Cagney

she retired from amateur skating and came to the United States that she truly became a star. Henie went on to make 11 Hollywood movies and to produce and skate in many musical extravaganzas on ice. For 13 of the 21 years during which her Hollywood Ice Revue toured, Henie was featured as the star. Henie's shows were noted for their elaborate costumes and skillful choreography, and her skating style was noted for athletic elements that previously had been unique to male competition. But her greatest contribution to the sport was to bring it to the public, transforming figure skating from a participants' sport into a spectator sport.

Celeste Holm, whose father was Norwegian, starred in many musical stage comedies, including *Oklahoma!*, *The King and I,* and *Mame.* Her movie performances were also acclaimed, and she won an Academy Award in 1947, for *Gentlemen's Agreement.* She also received Oscar nominations for her work in the films *Come to the Stable* and *All About Eve.*

Sonja Henie was both an entertainer and an athlete. She dominated women's amateur figure skating for more than a decade, winning Olympic gold medals for her native Norway in 1928, 1932, and 1936. She also won six European gold medals, as well as 10 championship skating titles. But it was when

Celeste Holm

Jan Stenerud

Knute Rockne (1888–1931), perhaps the greatest coach in American college football, was born in the little village of Voss in southern Norway. He came to America with his parents in 1893 and grew up in Chicago. As a chemistry student at the University of Notre Dame, he starred on the school's football team as team captain. After graduating in 1914, Rockne became a chemistry instructor at the university and assistant football coach. He was promoted to head football coach at Notre Dame in 1918 and over the next 13 seasons was nationally known for his record of 105 wins, 12 losses, and 5 ties. Rockne developed an approach to football that emphasized speed, agility, and deception in offensive play. Rockne's winning record and colorful personality made him a national celebrity. He remained at Notre Dame until his death in an airplane accident in 1931.

Jan Stenerud, born and raised in Norway, came to the United States on a skiing scholarship. Yet he pursued a career in football and came to be considered the finest and most consistent placekicker in the history of the National Football League. Kicking the football soccer style, a method that most placekickers have since adopted, Stenerud played 19 seasons without missing a game. Thirteen of those years were with the Kansas City Chiefs, four with the Green Bay Packers, and the last two with the Minnesota Vikings. He retired in 1985 at the age of 43, after 373 field goals (an NFL record) and 1,699 points. In January of 1991, Stenerud was elected to the Pro Football Hall of Fame.

INDEX

ACKNOWLEDGMENTS The photographs in this book are reproduced through the courtesy of: p. 2, American Birkebeiner; pp. 6, 9, 31, 33, 41, The Library of Congress; pp. 7, 28, Lynn Olsen; pp. 8, 10, 14, 15, 16, 17, 18, 39, 57, Independent Picture Service; p. 11, Viking Research, Bill Holman, Alexandria, Minnesota; pp. 12, 13, Canadian Parks Service; p. 20, Sons of Norway; p. 21, G. Bratvold; pp. 22, 26, 29, 35, 42, 70, 71, Liv Dahl; pp. 25, 49, 50, 52, 53, 59, Minnesota Historical Society; p. 27, Norwegian-American Museum, Decorah, Iowa; p. 32, K. Knudsen and Company for National Theater, Bergen, Norway; p. 34, Weyerhauser Company; p. 37, Anundsen Publications Company; p. 40, Loren Paulson, Sons of Norway; pp. 43, 44, USDA Photo; p. 45, The Rockefeller Foundation; p. 46, Medtronic, Inc.; p. 47, The Port Authority of New York and New Jersey; p. 48, Woolworth Corporation; p. 51, Office of Senator Hubert H. Humphrey; p. 54, Office of Representative Martin Olav Sabo; p. 56 (top), Sidney L. Webb; p. 56 (bottom), University of Cincinnati; p. 58, CBS News Photo; p. 60, John Danicic, Jr.; p. 61, Leo Holub; p. 62, Jerry Bauer, HarperCollins; p. 63, St. Olaf College Archives, St. Olaf College; p. 64, The Metropolitan Opera; p. 65 (top and bottom), 20th Century-Fox Film Corp.; p. 66, Minnesota Vikings Football Club, Rick A. Kolodziej; p. 69 (left), Hilton Hotels Corporation; p. 69 (right), University of Notre Dame.

Front cover photograph: Liv Dahl. Back cover photographs: The Rockefeller Foundation (left); Jerry Bauer, HarperCollins (upper right); 20th Century-Fox Film Corp. (lower right).

Conrad Hilton

Knute Rockne

American tourists in Norway visit a popular attraction, Oslo's Frogner Park. The sculpture garden displays about 150 pieces from the work of 20th-century expressionist artist Gustav Vigeland.

Immigrants to the United States from Norway 1820 to 1990

1820	3*
1821-1830	91*
1831-1840	1,201*
1841-1850	13,903*
1851-1860	20,931*
1861-1870	71,631
1871-1880	95,323
1881-1890	176,586
1891-1900	95,015
1901-1910	190,505
1911-1920	66,395
1921-1930	68,531
1931-1940	4,740
1941-1950	10,100
1951-1960	22,935
1961-1970	15,484
1971-1980	3,941
1981-1990	4,164
Total	801,224

* For the years 1820-1860, the immigration figures for Norway and Sweden are combined.

Source: Immigration and Naturalization Service, U.S. Department of Justice

THE *IN AMERICA* SERIES

Lerner Publications Company
241 First Avenue North • Minneapolis, Minnesota 55401